Prayers
for Catholics
Experiencing Divorce

Prayers for Catholics Experiencing Divorce

VICKI WELLS BEDARD
AND WILLIAM E. RABIOR

Liguori

LIGUORI, MISSOURI

Imprimi Potest:
Richard Thibodeau, C.Ss.R.
Provincial, Denver Province
The Redemptorists

Imprimatur:
Most Reverend Robert J. Hermann
Auxiliary Bishop of St. Louis

Published by Liguori Publications
Liguori, Missouri
www.liguori.org

Library of Congress Cataloging-in-Publication Data

Bedard, Vicki Wells.
    Prayers for Catholics experiencing divorce / Vicki Wells Bedard and William E. Rabior.— Rev. ed.
        p. cm.
    ISBN 0-7648-1156-8
    1. Divorced people—Prayer-books and devotions—English. 2. Divorce—Religious aspects—Catholic Church—Prayer-books and devotions—English. 3. Catholic Church—Prayer-books and devotions—English. I. Rabior, William E. II. Title.

BX2170.D55B43 2004
242'.846—dc22   2003065860

Printed in the United States of America
08 07 06 05 04   5 4 3 2 1
Revised edition 2004

Dedicated
with much love
to Paige, Zachary, Joshua,
Chloe, Sam, and Gabrielle.

Thank you
for all the light and laughter
you have brought to us.

Contents

Prayer
for the Pray-ers

Good and gracious God,
  Bless all those you bring to these pages,
    all who share the common denominator
    of having experienced divorce.

Most are hurting, God.
  Heal their hurt.
    Many are enraged at what has happened to them.
      Calm their rage.
    Some are anxious and depressed.
      Soothe their troubled minds and emotions.
    All are injured and in need of healing.
      Touch them; heal them.

May you, God, who knows us intimately—
  and from whom nothing can be hidden—
    enlighten and direct
    all those drawn to this book.
  Help them find peace.
  Help them find the renewal of mind
    and spirit they seek.
Bring rest to their tired hearts, O God.
  Dispel their darkness of despair,
    and bathe them in the light of new hope.

As they communicate with you through these prayers,
    may they also communicate
    with their deepest selves
    to discover who they are
    and how valuable they are.
May they draw closer to you
    the Source of all human identity.

Bless them well, life-giving God.
    Bless and heal them as only you can.

Amen

Luke Thiele Bedard

William Rabior

PART I

From Coupleness to Singleness

Genesis II

God, my friend,
   "For this reason a man shall leave his father and
   mother and be joined to his wife,
   and the two shall become one flesh" (Matthew 19:5).
      The two shall become one.
         It's funny, Lord.
            I was once two and am now one again—
            one in this two-for-the-price-of-one world.
            I hardly know where to begin.
When I married, did I substitute taking care of myself,
      for taking care of both of us?
            Maybe—maybe.
   Maybe things would be easier
      if there were a second version of Genesis:
      "And this is why one spouse
      leaves and clings to whatever he or she can,
      and the one left takes possession of
      what's left
      like custody of children, debts,
               and other responsibilities,
         and loses possession of sanity."
            But there is no Genesis II.

It isn't easy, Lord.
   Becoming a single in a "couple" society and Church;
      finding a place to fit in.
            The task seems overwhelming.
   Am I a failure?
      Some seem to think so.

Even I think that—
sometimes.
Am I competent enough to make decisions for myself,
to establish a new life and lifestyle?
I don't know.
I don't even know how I got here.
I didn't get married to become divorced.
I married for a lifetime, just the two of us
facing the world together.
A romantic idea—
but for us, not realistic.

That's what I need to remember, God, my friend.
I must now define my life with something unique,
something special only to me this time:
not to my family,
not to my former spouse,
not to my friends.
Help me with this.
Together, let's rediscover who I am.
Growth is not experienced without change
and sometimes a loss of what's familiar.
"Unless a seed falls to the ground and dies,
there can be no fruit."
I have heard you say that so many times.
But today,
I hear it for the first time.
I have to let go of the past
and hold out my arms to you.

Together, let's write my future, God.
                                        Amen

Divorce Hurts

Divorce hurts, God!
   It hurts in lots of ways, mostly in my mind and spirit.
      When I think about what has happened,
         I often feel terrible; I even hate myself at times.
         I feel like dirt.
         I blame myself.
      During times like these, I need you the most.
      When I talk to you,
         I don't feel the condemnation or criticism
         that cuts through my soul
         and messes up my mind.
      Rather, I feel loved,
            accepted,
            understood,
            forgiven.
   Although I may see myself as having "failed,"
      you never label me as anything
         but love.
   Divorce does not make me a bad person
      or an unforgivable sinner. I am human—
         and I need you.

Right now, I'm one of the walking wounded,
      recovering from the damage of divorce.
         But the wounds will heal, and I will be whole again.

Love me back to life, God.
Transform my pain and self-pity
into something good and useful.
When I start beating on myself,
tell me to stop.
Whisper love to my soul.

With your help, I'm going to make it, God.
I'm not giving up.
I'm moving on and choosing to hope.
Go with me, God.
Amen

My Dream Has Died

Dear God,
   I never wanted my wonderful dream to die:
      a close, loving family,
      sharing intimacy,
      growing old together.
   There is nothing wrong with that dream.
   But when the dream started to unravel,
      the nightmare began.
   How I mourn the death of my dream;
      I long to wake up from the nightmare
         to find everything like it used to be:
         my marriage and family intact,
         the emotional hurricane
            only part of a restless night.
   But the emotional hurricane is a reality;
      my marriage is over,
      and nothing is going to change that.

Good God, I need a new dream.
   I need a brand-new dream for me—
      a shining-star dream,
      one that will guide the way into my future.

You, God, are the original dream-maker.
   Through the gentle touch of your Spirit,
      put a new dream into my mind,
               my heart,
               my spirit.
                        Amen

This Is Not a Broken Home

Dear God,
    The "broken home" is one of the stereotypes
      associated with divorce.
        Well, my marriage may be ended,
          but my home is not broken.
        Its composition is different, yes,
          but we remain a family,
            not a deficient family,
            not an inadequate family,
            not a broken home.

Our new home will be characterized
   by as much love and loyalty
   as we can bring to it.
      By our hard work and dedication to one another,
        we are going to make this
        as genuine and true a home
        as any home anywhere.

God, bless our new home and all of us in it.
   Show us how to enrich our relationships,
             to draw closer to one another,
             to make this a place of healing
               and peace.
   Our commitment as a family did not end with divorce.
     We were a family; we are a family.
     Nothing will change that.

With your help and grace,
    and with us helping one another,
    we're going to do just fine.

Watch out, world, here we come—
    new and improved
        and forever a family!

           Amen

Holidays Are Hard

Lord,
 Holidays are hard.
  Whether it be Thanksgiving Day, Christmas, Easter,
   or the Fourth of July,
   holidays feel different.
 The difference isn't necessarily bad;
   it's strange,
   uncomfortable,
   awkward with nostalgia.

Holidays release a flood of memories.
 Some good, some terrible,
  all vivid.
 It's as though I am watching a home movie:
  there we all are,
  doing the traditional things—making memories.

Depending upon the holiday,
 I may feel empty or elated,
   lonely or lucky,
   hollow or happy.
 In any event,
  holidays present a special emotional challenge.

I have shed many a holiday tear since the divorce, Lord,
 I have wallowed in self-pity and rage,
 I have been preoccupied with pain.

Too often I have ignored the needs of others,
     even those closest to me.
Holidays remind me that my grieving is not over yet.

Continue your healing work within me, Lord Jesus.
   Help me through the special events.
   Teach me to tune into the pain of others,
               to be a friend,
               to soothe the holiday aches of others,
               to find my own healing in the love of others.
With your guidance
and with an awareness of your presence,
     I long for the holidays
          —and all my days—
          to be holy days,
          days to love and serve you
                    by loving and serving others.
                              Amen

Absent Without Leave

[AWOL]

Lord,
   I miss my children.
      Not a day goes by that I don't wonder
         what they're doing,
         what they're thinking,
         what I'm missing.
   When I see them,
      I'm startled at how much they've changed.

I want them to love me, Lord.
   I want them to miss me.
   I want them to jump up and down when they see me.
Sometimes they do, Lord,
         …and sometimes they don't.
      Sometimes I'm overjoyed.
         …and sometimes I'm disappointed.
   I wonder if I am a good parent, a good person.
      I wonder.
   I remember the times I've wanted my former spouse
     to know loneliness the way I do,
    to feel rejection as I have felt it.
      But I know the children need a stable home.
       I know we can't divide up children
         like we do property.
           Yes, I'm a good parent.

I remember, too, when I've been tempted
  to buy my children's affections,
  to be the family Santa Claus,
  the good fairy and the perfect parent.
And it's so hard to discipline the children
  when I see them so rarely.
  I want their acceptance and approval,
    yet allowing them to do and say anything
      isn't love.
        It's manipulation.
We all lose
  when I cannot be the parent, only the buddy.
    Yes, I'm a good parent.

We are all joined to you, Lord.
  We are a family through you.
    Help me cut the distance between me and my children
      with phone calls,
      with letters,
      with my presence when they need me.
    Help me make separation a fruitful experience
        and may I be grateful for that.
    Because I am the "reserves"—
        fresh and not war-weary—
    I can be objective.
    I can see humor when it seems hard to find.
    I can see goodness when it seems absent.
    I can be supportive.
    I can pray for them always.
    I can love them and ease their burdens.

                                        Amen

For Guidance

Lord and Friend,
    Being alone is difficult.
        I have no one who will listen to me,
                no one who will offer loving advice.
        And yet, I always have you; I am your child.
           With the trusting faith of a child,
                I come to you now with this special concern:
                (Mention your need.)

I ask for your guidance and direction, dear God.
    Because I am your beloved child,
        I pray with full confidence;
        I know you want what is best for me.
        I know you will direct and lead as only you can.
    Because your Holy Spirit is present to me,
        I can let go of any anxiety about this matter.
        I place it entirely in your hands
           and await your peace—
           the peace that surpasses all understanding.

As you have loved me,
        as you have been my light along the way,
        may I be a light for others,
        helping them in their life's journey.

Thank you for hearing me, God.
    I pray, as always, in the name of Jesus,
        the Lord and light of our world.
                        Amen

For My Finances

Bountiful God,
   Once again, I face too much month
      and not enough money.
         Since my divorce, managing my finances
            has become an ongoing struggle.
   Increasingly, it seems, I have less money
      and more—so many more—financial demands.
   Although I try to be careful,
      my financial resources get rapidly depleted.
         I become anxious;
         I panic.
   When I feel that way, I need to anchor myself in you.
   You, who take care of the lilies of the field,
      can certainly take care of me and my needs.

Guide me in wise use of financial resources, God.
      Although my resources are limited,
         may I budget wisely,
         always sensitive to the needs
         of those who have even less than I.
   I believe that in giving, I receive.
   I believe that in your generous providence,
      the work of my hands will prosper.

For all your blessings to me and my family,
   thank you, gracious God.
                                    Amen

For the Memories

Lord,
    The human mind is a mighty and terrible thing—
        mighty wonderful or terribly sad.
            My mind isn't of the mighty, wonderful variety
            right now.
                My mind
                is playing tricks on me.
    All the reasons I left this marriage,
        good reasons and poor reasons,
            seem to escape me.
    I miss being a couple.
    My mind is trying to say, "You have made a mistake."
      It doesn't matter that I cannot go back.
      It doesn't matter that I have changed,
        my former spouse has changed,
        our families have changed,
        our children have changed.
                It still feels like a mistake.

At times, I remember the ugly things,
    the failures and fights,
    the anger and arguments,
    the silent "you-win-again" losses—
        and I feel like I'm the "good guy."
At other times, I remember the good things,
    the trips and traditions,
    the laughter and love,
    the "we-can-work-it-out" determination—
        and I feel like I'm the "bad guy."

What began all this, Lord?
Sure, I'm tired;
I'm *always* tired.
Was it a bad day? There are a lot of them.
Am I feeling rejected, neglected?
All of the above—
plus I'm lonely.
I know my marriage wasn't all good or all bad.
I really do know that;
I really do believe that.
But sometimes my memory replays stories,
stories about things that never happened.
In looking back, I see a vivid technicolor marriage,
not the muted, then black and white,
reruns it had become.
Was I happy then and didn't see it? didn't know it?
Have I lost something really terrific?
Can't I find a way to get back there
or at least find someone else
so I don't have to keep trying so hard?

Lord, what did I just say?
I'm living in the past to avoid the future!
Why didn't I realize that before?

My friend, talking with you
never ceases to amaze me.
Right before my eyes, with my own words,
I see what you are helping me to see.
Memories are okay!
And, oh, I do have a lot of wonderful memories.
Help me keep them in focus—and in perspective.

As for the bad memories, I turn them over to you.
Heal me of them so that I may set them aside
to make room for new ones,
memories that I am in charge of,
memories I can proudly point to and say,
"I made that decision...all by myself...
okay, with a little help from you, my friend."
Amen

When I'm Simply Lonely

Hi, Lord Jesus,
I want to talk to you about the way I'm feeling right now.
 I'm not having a bad day;
   in fact, things have been going reasonably well.
 All things considered, life is pretty good.

And yet, Lord, I am lonely—simply lonely.
 I know it's not the end of the world to be lonely.
 This will pass, and I will be just fine;
   but it's the way I feel right now—lonely and a little sad.
I want to be wanted, needed, and loved,
   but instead I feel isolated and alone.

I know there were times when you felt the very same way—
   times when you felt like crying, too.
 In the Garden of Gethsemane,
   your heart must have been breaking
   with loneliness and feelings of abandonment.
You know what I'm going through right now.
You know what it's like to have this hollow feeling
   deep inside.
 Sometimes even when I'm surrounded by others,
   I still feel it.

Anyway, Lord, with you by my side,
   I can never be truly alone.
 And I know, too, there are others all around me
   just as lonely as I am.

Send me to those who need me
   and send others to me,
      so that we can support and help one another.
And remind me, dear Friend,
      that you are always there for me—
         only a prayer away,
         so that when I'm simply lonely,
            I can simply turn to you.

                              Amen

Prayer Promise

Good and Gracious God,
   In and through this prayer
      I make a promise to you and to myself.
   I promise to strive with all that is within me
         to heal the hurts from my divorce experience.

   I will not allow myself to be emotionally crippled.
   I will not be maimed by what has happened.
   I will not be a victim.

God, I am going to get through this.
   I am going to get through this—with your help—
      restored, renewed, and re-created.
   I'm going to be a better person,
      living a better life.
   I will not wallow in pain.
   I reject self-pity and self-hatred;
      I may become discouraged—
            but not damaged.

Strengthened and supported by your grace and love,
  along with my own determination, God,
           I will heal.
   I will become a healthy, happy, and whole person.
        This I promise—
        to you
        and to myself.
                      Amen

PART II

From Loss
to Acceptance

Healing Takes Time

Loving God,
    I know that time doesn't heal all wounds,
      but all wounds require time to heal.
    I'm still hurting inside,
           grieving.
      I know I need more time.
      I need time to let go of the past,
         the deep-seated anger,
         the bitterness,
         the haunting guilt,
         the sense of personal failure,
      I need time to let go of my old identity,
           to form a new one—
           with your help.

Slow me down, God.
    Help me remember that there is no way
      to speed up the healing process.
      I need to be patient with myself.
      I need to realize that if I try to rush the process,
         I may have to repeat certain steps all over again—
         and I don't want that to happen.

With the help of your grace, dear God,
         I want to do it right.
    I want to heal thoroughly and completely
      and get on with life.
    I know that's something you want for me, too.

Above all, may I never forget
    that time spent with you in prayer
        is healing time.
As I come to know you better,
    may I also come to know myself better.
        Show me who I am.
        Co-create with me a new and better life,
            a life that is built on the wisdom of
            previous mistakes and pitfalls.
And even though I'm still wounded and hurting,
    use me to bring love and goodness into the world,
        to help others as best as I can,
        in spite of the fact
        that I'm in need
            of help and healing myself.

I'm far from being whole, God,
    yet, I thank you and praise you
        for bringing me this far,
        for the fullness of healing I will someday experience.
            I leave myself open to you
                so you may restore me
                and renew me
                    in ways only you
                    can accomplish.

                                        Amen

Befriending Myself

Lord Jesus,
    There's one important skill that I never learned
    before I was married or while I was married—
    a skill I need to learn now:
        how to make friends
        with myself.

For so long I have neglected myself,
    ignored my own needs and desires,
    hidden my dreams away.
For such a long time I relied on others,
    expected someone else to take care of me.

Now I know that I have to take care of myself.
    I want to learn that.
    I want to learn
        to treat myself like an old and dear friend
        who has just come back into my life.
    I want to be good and kind to myself.

My new life, wherever it takes me,
        begins with me—
        befriending me and becoming my own best friend.

Ah, but Jesus,
    that does not mean
        there is no room for you in my life.
        You have always been my friend.

Through the darkest,
    most painful days of my divorce,
        you were there for me.
You are closer to me
        than I am to myself.

Teach me how to be gentle with myself,
        how to stop being so harsh with myself,
        how to be less critical of myself.
Help me to be patient with myself,
    to affirm myself,
    to make myself strong,
    especially in weak and broken places.

Renew my thinking, Lord,
        renew my emotions and my attitudes.
    With the help of your grace,
    may I experience deep inner healing—
        mind and soul healing.
    As my friendship with myself develops and grows,
        may our friendship deepen and grow as well.
    In every sense of the word,
        I want you to be my soul mate
            for a lifetime
            and forever.

                              Amen

Lord, I'm Depressed

Lord Jesus,
   I feel as though only a small part of me remains alive—
      and I'm not even sure
      I want that part to go on living.
   Things look so hopeless, and I feel so helpless.
      People ask me "What's wrong,"
         and I can't even give them an intelligent answer.
   My mind doesn't seem to work right anymore.
      All I want to do is cry…and sleep.
         Nothing interests me
               except brooding about my pain.
   All I see behind me is a long trail of failures,
      failures that leave the present
         full of pain and uncertainty,
      failures that leave the future…
         I can't even bear
         to think about that.

Life has become too hard for me, Lord.
   I feel totally defeated,
             utterly empty.
   To be completely honest,
      I'm not sure I want to go on.
   Yet, a tiny voice inside of me says,
         "Go on.
         You must go on.
         You can go on."
   It's a voice that calls me out of the darkness
         into the light.

I believe it is your voice, Lord Jesus,
for you are no stranger to depression.
In Gethsemane and on the cross,
you experienced the savage feelings of
abandonment;
you knew the darkness of depression.
You know my feelings.
You know how the mind and soul overflows with pain.
You understand.

I know that this depression is dangerous, Lord.
It makes me believe that I'm helpless,
that I am incapable of changing my life,
that nothing good is going to happen to me anymore,
that I don't deserve anything good anyway.
This depression magnifies
everything I've ever done wrong,
every failure I've ever experienced,
every personal flaw I've ever identified.
This depression lies to me.
…and I'm tempted
to believe the lie.

Help me, Lord, to start fighting back.
Show me where to start.
Should I turn to my pastor?
my doctor?
my therapist?
all three?
Let me draw on their strength
and professional guidance.

Silence the prideful voice within me that says,
   "Ah, come on, you can conquer this by yourself."
      I know I can't.

Teach me, Lord, how to change my depressive thinking,
         thinking that is negative and bleak,
         filled with distortions.
      Fill me with optimism and hope.
      Reintroduce me to the simple pleasures of living:
         the invigoration of a long walk,
         the beauty of a flower,
         the music in a child's laughter.

I want to be a modern-day Lazarus, Lord.
   Call me forth from the tomb
      that my depression has created;
   call me to new life and renewed hope.
            I'm ready to live again!
            I mean it with all my heart.
   With your help,
      I will make it happen.

Resurrect me, Lord. I'm ready.
                              Amen

Into-Me, See?

God, my dearest friend,
   I once heard a child say that being close to another
      is called "into-me, see"—intimacy!
   You and I share intimacy;
         you know me;
         you know me from before I began.
   You know from the slightest alteration in my breathing
                  that I am bored,
                  frightened, amused,
                  or deep in thought.
      We are perfect together,
                  you and I, Lord.
   You are accepting.
      Even after reading the hidden chapters of my heart,
            you love me still.

Maybe it's my love for you, Lord,
   that makes me want to find someone,
      someone with whom I can share "into-me, see"—
                  intimacy.
   I will never be able to share what we share,
      but I long to share something more human,
      less predictable.
   A part of Eastern philosophy says
      that love is what happens
      when two bodies share one soul.
         That's similar to what you said:
            "It is not good for man [woman] to be alone."
            You understand that.

Yet, I'm afraid to allow another to get close to me.
    After all, I didn't fare too well
        the last time I tried it.

I never understood the "new morality,"
    but I think I'm beginning to.
        Sometimes it is easier to share
            our saggy, wrinkled bodies
            than our saggy, wrinkled emotions and thoughts.
        It's easy to think that physical intimacy
            will lead to emotional closeness.
                But it isn't true.

Bonding begins from my neck up.
            Laughter,
            sharing secrets,
            being ornery (and sweet, of course),
            allowing myself to be vulnerable and open,
            divulging my deepest thought or best joke:
                that is the beginning
                of intimacy.

Thank you, God, for sending someone special to me.
        You know I need a friend.
        You know I need someone to see into me,
            to grow with me as a person,
                as a precious child of yours.
        I believe you will provide that person for me.
        When that special person does see into me,
            may they see you.
                That would be a perfect union.
                        Amen

Certain Songs
Drive Me Crazy!

Dear Lord,
Certain songs drive me crazy!
When I hear old songs—
songs that remind me of yesterday,
of unfulfilled dreams—
it feels as if my heart and mind will burst.
Some days, every song I hear seems directed at me.
Since the divorce, I've gained a deeper respect
for the power of music:
it can calm and soothe me,
it can cur into my soul like a surgeon's scalpel.

I know I'm vulnerable and supersensitive right now.
Many of my feelings and emotions are still raw.
I have a lot of healing to do.

Remind me, Lord,
that it's all right to have these feelings—
even the powerful ones
that rise up like a tidal wave and engulf me.
If I don't feel, I won't heal,
and I want to heal!

I have cried, still cry, and will continue to cry.
Tears are a healing release.
Hold me when I cry, Lord;
hold me until the pain passes.
Amen

For My Future

God of mercies,
  I get terrified when I think about my future.
   Will I end up alone, with no one to love me?
  In my panic, I actually begin to believe
   that I'll be abandoned by everyone.

When these feelings and thoughts come, Lord,
 I want to run and hide; I don't want to face the future.
  Sadly, fear of my future
   makes the present unbearable,
    so I just can't win.

"Be not afraid."
 I hear your living word in the Scriptures.
  You invite me to have greater confidence in you.
  You tell me not to fear the future
   because the future belongs to you.
 That doesn't mean I can be passive and do nothing.
  I must work as though everything depends on me
   and pray as though everything depends on you.

Help me, Lord, to monitor my attitudes about the future.
 I can face it with dread
  or with determination and delight.
 Because I see your hand at work in my past,
  I choose to face the future with you.
 I welcome you as Lord of my future, Lord of my life
  …always and forever.
       Amen

For My Children

God, my parent,
There are so many things I wanted for my children:
good health,
education,
success,
happiness,
prosperity,
fun.
Wanted? I still want them.
I want all the good things for them *now*
that I wanted for them when they were born.
But I don't know how to do that by myself.
I'm overwhelmed.
How do I explain to my kids
that there isn't the money,
the time,
nor the energy
to do all the things we once did?
I can't accept that myself.
How do I face their disappointment
when other kids get what they want?
How do I watch their embarrassment
at no-name clothes and hand-me-downs?
How do I see the envy in their faces
as they watch the other kids' moms and dads
sitting together in the bleachers?
Sometimes I can't even get there at all—
let alone sit in the bleachers.

Lord, you know I never meant to hurt them,
    never meant to make them suffer or want.
        Neither of us did.
    We were young and in love
      and had the world gift-wrapped,
        ready to give our children all the good things.
        Divorce hurts.
        I hurt.
        They hurt.
        I'm sorry.

"You are precious, you are cherished, and I love you."
    Is that what I hear you saying to me?
    Is that what I need to say to my children?
      "Let's not worry about material things, kids.
      They will come in time.
      When you're old enough,
        you can earn those things.
      Working can be a gift, you know,
        feeling good
        about what you're able to get for yourself.
      Feeling important
        as a participating member of this family
          is a gift."

The children can help me put up storm windows,
      rake leaves,
        decorate for holidays.
    We can tell stories about the old days.
    We can dream of tomorrow.
    We can laugh…and cry.

We are rich with one another.
We are at a fresh beginning.
We can fashion this family any way we want.
We can build it on sorrow and remorse—
or we can build it on hope.

Nothing is impossible, God,
with you as our parent.

Amen

God, Me, and the Church

God, my friend,
    You have always accepted me just as I am.
    You rejoiced with me in the good times,
        sustained me through the bad.
    We are close;
        we are joined together since before my time.

I wish I could find that same sense of you
    within the structure of my Church.
The community that welcomed me at my birth,
        rejoiced at my baptism,
        applauded my first Communion,
        welcomed my repentance,
        blessed my confirmation,
        and witnessed my journey into marriage
            seems to have forgotten me.
I have become a misfit
    in an institution
    that places high regard for intact,
        two-parent families.
To be human is to expect change,
        to lose,
        to recover,
        to grow,
        to stumble,
        to begin anew.
It seems all those things are acceptable
    while we're married.

But should we feel called to a different response—
    to separate or divorce—
    we are...what?
        Suddenly less than human?

Lord, help this Church that I love,
    that helped me grow into adulthood.
Soften her heart.
Help her reach out to those of us who are
        alienated,
        hurt,
        or broken by life.
Help her find ways to offer us healing and peace.
Help her set aside judgments,
        hear our pain,
        hold our fear.
Help her reach out to us,
    not out of some code of law
    but out of genuine compassion
        and Christlike love.
The divorcing process surrounds us with laws;
    let it be the Church that surrounds us
        with love and mercy.

My sinfulness is not in leaving my marriage,
    for sometimes
        the kindest act of all
        is in letting go of another.
Let my Church see this.
Let my Church be sensitive to my singleness
    and the pain I endured as I arrived here.

I am not a half couple, Lord.
　　I am intact,
　　I am your creation.
　　I am your beloved.
　　　　And I hurt.
　　　　I fear rejection.
　　Please let your Church
　　　　embrace my hurt and rejection
　　　　and allow her to love me
　　　　as you love me.

Teach me, too, Lord,
　　to support those who minister to me.
　　Help me to help them understand.

Above all, dear God, let me remember,
　　as intimidating as the Church can be,
　　it is still comprised of human beings.
　　Some persons will be loving;
　　　some will be callous;
　　　some will fall in-between.
　　If I ask to be understood in my humanity,
　　　then I must apply the same measure in return.
　　　Show me how.
　　　　　　　　　　　Amen

One Year After My Divorce

Dear God,
This is an important anniversary:
one year—and I'm still here!
I didn't disintegrate,
evaporate,
or self-destruct.
There is life after divorce, and I'm living proof.
I'm a survivor who is not just surviving;
in many ways, I'm thriving.
I still have bad days;
I still feel pain.
But I haven't given up or given in to the despair
that dogged my heels for so long.
Day by day, I'm rebuilding my life,
rediscovering new meaning,
creating a new purpose.
I've made it this far, and with your help,
I'll keep making it, God.
Thank you for everything.

I never thought that the present and future
would actually look promising again—
but they do!

Thanks a lot, God.
Now help me keep my eyes on you
as I keep on moving forward and growing.
Amen

When Will I Ever Fit In?

God,
  There are moments when I feel I don't belong anywhere.
  As soon as I got my divorce, I became invisible,
      ignored and overlooked by people
          whom I thought would be there for me, but weren't—
          my friends, my coworkers, my community,
          and worse yet, my Church.
In this society that emphasizes couples,
  I feel like an out-of-place outsider—
      a stranger in a strange land.
The temptation is to give up and give in
      and simply withdraw,
      to disappear into my aloneness.
Yet, I know I cannot do that. I won't do that!
  I am going to seek until I find,
      knock until a door opens,
      until I fit in someplace.
There is a place for me, and I'm going to find it.
  I am not going away. I am a force to be reckoned with.
      If I can't find the right niche, then I'll create one myself.

Thank you, God, that I can come to you just as I am
          and be loved and accepted by you unconditionally.
      I belong to you right now,
          and I wish to belong to you for all eternity.
In your kingdom, the kingdom of heaven,
      there's a place for me where I will fit in forever.
          That's what salvation is all about, isn't it?
                                    Amen

For Greater Self-Love

Dear Lord,
    I can be so harsh, so severe with myself.
        I make demands of myself—
            demands I would never make of others—
            demands I would never make of me.
    Then, when I can't live up to my own expectations,
        I become my worst critic.
    I have a motto:
        "I have met the enemy, and the enemy is myself."

    I don't know how I got to be this way, Lord.
        Many factors must have converged
            to form this harsh self-outlook.
        This I do know, though,
            I want to change.
    I want to love me in a healthy, positive way.

    Show me how to do this, Lord.
        Help me remove the obstacles to healthy self-love.
        Teach me how to be gentle with myself,
        to love myself; for in loving myself,
            I love others.
        In loving myself, I become the healed
            and the healer.
You have loved me with an everlasting love, Lord Jesus.
    Help me believe in and absorb that love
    so I can better love myself and others.
                    Amen

PART III

From Pain
to Peace

Healing Is Happening!

Good Lord,
    I seem to be having more good days than bad.
    I feel like I'm being brought from a place of pain
             to a place of peace.
        I'm finding new direction,
          new purpose,
          new meaning—
             even joy!

Good signs, Lord, very good signs, indeed.
    The pain inside isn't as intense as it once was,
        and I can feel the broken places starting to mend.
    I'm beginning to heal,
           and it feels wonderful!

Thanks, Lord, for whatever you are doing
  to help this process along.
             Please keep
             the healing happening.
                   Amen

God, I'm Sorry I Divorced You

Dear God,
    As I went through my divorce,
        I had a lot of anger—
                especially at you.
        In fact, I think I was probably more angry at you
            than I've been willing to admit in the past.
        There were times, in fact,
            when I actually felt more rage at you
            than at my former spouse.
        I guess that I expected you somehow—
                miraculously—
            to do something
            that would make everything right.
        When I didn't get my miracle,
            I decided that my relationship with you
            wasn't that crucial.
                So I divorced you.

But I've changed, Lord.
    There's been too much emptiness deep inside;
        nothing and no one has been able to fill it.
    I want to come back to you.
    I want to make a fresh start with you.
    I want things to be normal again.
                I need you.

I can see now
that you never divorced me or abandoned me.
You were there all the time, waiting—
waiting for me
to come to my senses,
to come back home to you.

You know, God, it's really hard to stay furious
at someone who treats you so well.
Forgive me.
I'm sorry.

And thank you, too, Lord—
for your patience,
for accepting me,
for being faithful to me,
even when I was at my worst.
Thank you for your understanding,
for your forgiveness,
and for your mercy.

Amen

It's Time to Let Go of Anger

Lord Jesus,
    I'm sick and tired of being angry.
      For a long while, it felt good,
             satisfying.
    I could get angry—and stay angry;
      I could sting my former spouse with that anger
        at every opportunity.
    In fact, anger has been a tonic for me.
      It helped me survive,
             kept me going,
             enabled me to get things done.
    When nothing else could or would motivate me,
             anger never failed.

During this healing time, Lord,
  I've learned that even righteous anger
  can be wrong,
          unhealthy,
          dangerous.
    Although my anger may have been entirely
             appropriate—
    perhaps even necessary at times—
             it no longer is.
    I know now that if I continue to stay angry,
      the anger will become my emotional master;
             I will be its slave.

It's time to let go, Lord.
     The rage no longer serves a purpose.
     Today, anger only makes me sad,
                              despondent,
                              downhearted.
          It ruins my day.

When I think about it, Lord,
     I realize that most of my anger went unnoticed
               by my former spouse.
          I was usually the only person it affected.
          While I sat at home stewing in my own juices,
          my spouse was totally unaware.

And so I'm learning, Lord, with your help.
     I'm learning to take away the control
          I've often given to that emotion.
     I realize that I'll probably have to pray this prayer
                    over and over again,
          because when I'm angry,
                    I obsess.
                    I magnify my past hurts.
                    I rekindle ancient rage.

I'm a slow learner, Lord, but I mean business here.
     I'm serious about ridding myself
          of this useless emotional baggage that weighs me down.
     Help me find peace and healing
               as I turn this anger over to you,
               as you lead me more and more
                    from rage to calm.
                                   Amen

Someone to Watch Over Me

Lord,
    I've begun to get my act together.
    I've had a string of good days.
    I've acted like a grownup.
    I've made my own decisions,
        cooked my own meals,
        paid my own bills,
        started and ended my own arguments.
      Not too bad for someone
        who's experienced a divorce.
      Not too bad at all.
           Or is it?

I thought I was independent, Lord.
    All the magazine articles say to plunge headlong
      into self-improvement plans:
        go to school,
        earn new degrees,
        "Learn to do everything yourself!"

But why? For example, widowhood isn't like that.
    A "surviving" mate can accept
        casseroles and condolences.
      The surviving mate can cry.
      The surviving mate can be
        cooking illiterate
        and mechanically illiterate—
          and it's okay.

Why isn't it okay to have those same responses
    when your spouse is divorced from you?
        Why do I have to do it all?
        What compels me to turn down offers of help,
            to refuse gifts of time,
                money,
                or other sundry items?
Even as a couple,
    I doubt we could have accomplished
        this long list of things—
        things that I'm now encouraged to accomplish alone.

God, I want to be allowed to be vulnerable.
    In this "I-can-do-it-all-by-myself" society,
        I forget that I can do nothing unless it's with you.
        From breathing to changing the oil,
            it all comes from you.

And I need to remember that it's okay
    to not want to do everything on my own.
        I can ask friends and family for help.
        I can accept gifts from people.
        I can allow others to be generous to me.
        I can even give myself permission to hire someone
            to do what I can't do
            or don't want to do.
        I remain a mature individual,
            able to grow and learn,
                to let go or hold on.

Most importantly, Lord, I can curl up next to you,
     use your shoulder,
        weep my tears into your robe.
  I can let you take complete control
     of all the areas of my life.
  Not only *can* I—
                    I must.

  It's okay to let go. It's okay to be weak.
     "Unless you become as little children
        you shall not enter the kingdom of God."

Lift me up, Lord, and hold me close.
  I do need someone to watch over me.
                    I am grateful that it's you.
                         Amen

Litany of Forgiveness

Dear God,
    Those who show pity but forget compassion,
                I forgive.
    Those who feel I have sinned,
        I am weak, or I am at fault,
                I forgive.
    Those who pull away from me—
        whether from their own confusion,
        their own embarrassment,
        their own sense of marital vulnerability,
        or their inability to speak to my pain,
                I forgive.
    Those who label me unlovable,
                I forgive.
    Those who see me as "too available"
        and assume I will participate in immoral behavior,
                I forgive.
    Those who reach out to the widowed
        with casseroles,
        inclusion in social activities,
        and deep expressions of sorrow—
            but forget my presence
            in that same lonely and confused community,
                I forgive.
    Those who make me the object of their gossip
        as they explore and distort my life story,
                I forgive.

The Church
  who sees me as neither married, single, nor divorced,
  who sees me as some faceless half couple,
  who labels me as a "failed marriage participant,"
  who finds the need to annul that which was
      once very dear to me,
        I forgive.
Society, as it labels my family "broken,"
        I forgive.
Friends who have left me for whatever reasons,
        I forgive.
Parents and children
  who are embarrassed and ashamed of my singleness
     and life choices,
        I forgive.
My absent spouse,
    to whom I am still tied by confusing emotions,
  who left me with a mixture of
    good and bad experiences and memories,
  who wounded and harmed me in very deep ways,
        I forgive.

Myself
  and whatever sense of personal failure
    I have appropriated,
      for my shortcomings,
      my very real humanity,
      my lapses into despair,
      my self-pity journeys,
      my unbridled anger,
      my discovery of jealousy, envy,

and other undesirable character traits,
    my desire to cling
        to unhealthy but familiar life patterns
        instead of looking with hope and trust to you,
            I forgive.

                          Amen

For My Former Spouse

Lord,
This is not an easy prayer.
When it comes to _____.
I have many mixed emotions.
Sometimes I feel I still love her/him.
Then, in the next moment,
I hate her/him.
At times, I care with all my heart
about what happens to _____;
at other times,
I couldn't care less!
I don't understand myself and my feelings
when it comes to this person with whom I shared
a part of my life.
But I do want to be able to pray for   .
Despite any turmoil or pain
that might remain in our relationship,
_____ remains a significant part of my life's story.

I lift _____ to you, O God,
I place her/him in your hands.
The funny thing is
I don't even know what to pray for,
what her/his needs are anymore.
But you do.
Take care of _____, as only you can.

As I have been absolved and forgiven by you,
I want to be able to absolve and forgive _____.
In whatever remains of our relationship,
I want there to be an absence of malice
and an abundance of peace.

Lord, this prayer is an important part
of my healing process.
Even as I desire to have a healed heart,
so, too, do I want _____ to have a healed heart.
I want both of us to be happy and whole persons.
We may never be friends again,
but I don't want us to be enemies, either.
So bless _____ in every area of life.
With the help of your grace,
may we both experience renewal and healing;
may we both find the strength to rebuild our lives.
Amen

For My Former In-Laws

Lord,
  I lift up my former in-laws to you in prayer this day.
    The common denominator we share together
      is that all of us have been hurt
      by the experience of divorce.
      The fallout from the divorce
      has contaminated our relationship in some ways.
  I guess that was to be expected.
    Yet—when all is said and done,
      I really do want what is best for them.
      I want to see healing and reconciliation
        take place between us.
    Although we no longer share the word *family*,
      we do not have to be estranged, bitter, or distant.
    I want, as far as it is possible,
      a warm and comfortable relationship with them.

Bless my in-laws, Lord, as only you can.
  Our relationship is going to be different now,
    but I want it to be characterized
                by peace,
                by understanding,
                by forgiveness,
                by love, and
                by your grace.
                          Amen

Grace Before Meals

Gracious God,
    As I pause for nourishment,
        I thank you for the ways you nourish and nurture me
        —not just through this food,
            but through family,
                friends,
                and friendship with you.
Bless and help those who have no food this day:
        the homeless and hungry
        and all those hurting in any way.
Through your goodness,
    I have been given this food to eat.
    I have also received blessings and graces
    beyond counting—most of which
        I will not comprehend or appreciate,
            until one day
                I see you face to face.

I am grateful, dear God, for all your many gifts.
    Above all, I am grateful for you,
                the giver,
                the source of all that I have
                and all that I am
                and all that I will ever be.

To you, God, we give praise, honor, and glory forever.
                        Amen

Meat Sale

God, my friend,
   It's a jungle out there.
      No, it's more like a meat market,
         a very expensive enterprise
         that threatens to make human dignity
         no more than a hunk of meat going for $1.19
            a pound—
               if that much.
   It's not that life isn't exciting,
      a crazy quilt of experiences.
         It's that today it's too crazy.
            Years ago when I met my former spouse,
            it seemed
               saner,
               quieter,
               safer.
That's it! Safer! It was a safer time.
   Young people met at high-school dances,
         college "mixers,"
         family reunions,
         neighborhood block parties,
         the church social hall.
   There was always someone
      who shared in your background or values,
         your hopes and dreams,
         your mutual adolescent failures.
   A pimple carried a conversation for hours.
   People didn't ask if you were HIV-positive—
         ever.

I grew up,
    got married to a wonderful person,
    settled down to create a family,
    and made married friends—
              friends who valued
              the same things we did.
Now, I'm divorced.
      There are no church social halls anymore,
        unless I count "Bingo."
      There are singles bars instead,
        singles clubs,
        and parents without partners.
I am sixteen all over again,
    but Mom and Dad aren't here
  to look over prospective beaus—
      or to tell me "no."

Lord, who changed the rules while I wasn't looking?
  Where am I to find someone special,
          someone unique,
  in this meat-market mentality?
I'm tired of leers that say
        "divorced = easy."
I want to socialize with someone,
      carry on a conversation,
      laugh—
      maybe dance—
      and not have to go to bed with the person.

Instead of friendship,
    society has substituted the word *performance*.
      Not just sexually
        but how we dress,
            laugh,
            our body image,
            and our body language.
    I feel on parade,
      in competition.

God, my all-knowing parent,
    I believe you want me to be happy.
    I believe you think I am lovable,
            deserve love,
            deserve companionship.
    So I put my faith in you.
      Even as this prayer is being said,
        you are sending someone to me,
              someone who will enrich my life,
              be my companion.

I thank you for this blessing, dear God.
    I will keep my eyes open and watch for that person.

Remind me, too, dearest friend,
  not to comprise myself
  or to put my price per pound beyond value—
    for I am precious,
      I am cherished,
      I am loved
            by you.
                      Amen

Poem Prayer

Thanks be to God,
  For tipsy flowers,
    drunk with rain,
      and velvet hours
         soft-spent, steeped in firelight.
  For robin eggs
   and pheasant flight.
  For sun
    and sun-soaked afternoons.
  For Sunday trips
   and red balloons
    and honest love in honest eyes.
  For mountain crags
   and baby cries.
  For all that glistens, glows and gleams—
   Christmas lights and crystal streams.
  For joy
   that peals out like a bell.
  And peace
   that whispers, "All is well."
  For hands that touch
   and smiles that care.
  For morning stars
   and evening prayer.
  For knowing, Lord,
   that you are there.

Thanks be to God!

                       Amen

What Is Your Plan
for My Life, God?

God of my past, present, and future,
   Sometimes I wish I were an arrow shot from your bow
      straight into my destiny, so that I get things just right—
         so that I do what you want me to do
         and become what you want me to be.
   I want my destiny to be perfectly fulfilled.

But I know that it doesn't work that way.
   Our life path doesn't go in a straight line.
   It is crooked—
      full of twists and turns,
      ups and downs,
      clarity and confusion.

My destiny is slowly unfolding daily,
   and I need to be patient—
      even though patience is a real struggle.

I also believe that you have not just one plan,
   but many plans for my life.
Each day brings teachable moments
      and creative challenges—
      moments and challenges that can draw me closer to you.
And that is what it is all about anyway,
      isn't it,
         drawing closer to you?

Working with you,
    may I become all I am meant to be;
  and in the becoming,
    may I know your peace and joy.
With your help,
    I truly believe the best is yet to come.
With your help,
    I will stay fit for this big, lifelong adventure,
    by walking with you, dear Friend.

                       Amen

PART IV

From
Darkness
to New Life

Litany of Mercy

Dear God,
    When I refuse to let go of the self-pity
        that prevents me from healing,
            Lord have mercy.
    When I deliberately hold on to and nurture
        rage, bitterness, and hatred
            toward my former spouse
        instead of working through
            and eliminating these feelings,
                Christ have mercy.
    When I neglect myself and my own needs,
            Lord have mercy.
    When I hold on to the pain of the past,
        savor it,
        when I should let go,
            Christ have mercy.
    When I refuse to work on the negative,
        hopeless,
        helpless thinking
        that keeps me depressed,
            Lord have mercy.
    When I backbite,
        spread rumors,
        and gossip
        about my former spouse,
            Christ have mercy.

When I wish my former spouse were dead,
            Lord have mercy.
When I wish I were dead,
            Christ have mercy.
When my stubbornness will not let me accept help
    when I desperately need it,
            Lord have mercy.
When I worry to the point of getting sick,
            Christ have mercy.
When I choose to remain miserable
    when I could just as well choose to be happy,
            Lord have mercy.
When I fail to become my own best friend
    and instead become my own worst enemy,
            Christ have mercy.
When I lust over genuine intimacy,
    when I misuse my gift of sexuality,
            Lord have mercy.
When I act childishly and immaturely
    instead of like the adult I am,
            Christ have mercy.
When I fail to reach out and help others
    who are also hurting and in need,
            Lord have mercy.
When I use my bad days as excuses
            for being unloving,
            uncaring,
            unkind,
            Christ have mercy.

When I choose self-hatred over self-love,
       Lord have mercy.
When I let my grief over the loss of my marriage
  become toxic and self-destructive,
       Christ have mercy.
When I blame others
  for my own inappropriate behavior,
   when I refuse to become responsible and mature,
       Lord have mercy.
When I fail to trust you,
    to follow your guidance and leading,
    to cherish our relationship,
    to return your love,
       Christ have mercy.
When I refuse to become the kind of person I can be
  with the help of your grace,
       Lord have mercy.
          Amen

Morning Offering

God of beginnings,
   The night has ended.
        Good God,
          it's morning!
  Wherever we were yesterday,
    it is behind me.
I ask you to help me
   retain the good thoughts
   and experiences from yesterday
      —and help me apply them to this day's growth.
This day is fresh,
     unmarked.
   It awaits my imprint.
   It is my gift to use for good
       or to waste.

I ask you, God,
     to help me organize and prioritize events of this day.
     Whatever this day holds,
       it is gift.
     There is nothing I will face
     that will not have you beside me,
        guiding me,
        directing me,
        protecting me.
    I am grateful
      for your presence.

I offer you all my thoughts,
>
> words,
>
> and actions,
>
> united with all your people throughout the world,
>
> with our living Eucharist, Jesus Christ,
>
> your son and our brother.

I ask your blessings on me
>
> and your particular intercession in…
>
> *(Mention a special intention.)*

I also ask you to remember those dear to me,
>
> especially…

Keep me from becoming stagnant, O God.
>
> When I'm tired, refresh me.
>
> Provide me with sustenance for this day.
>
> Allow me opportunities to be generous,
>
> knowing as I give, I shall receive.

Keep my mind alert,
>
> my eyes clear,
>
> my heart and head aligned.

Keep me aware of all the opportunities
>
> this day will bring,
>
> this day of promise
>
> and new beginnings.

Amen

Evening Prayer

God, my friend,
    Thank you for walking with me today.
        It is comforting to know that you are
           always with me,
           always watching me,
           always rejoicing over me—
                always.
        It is comforting to know that I am never alone.

Sometimes I reach this time of the evening
    exhausted and discouraged.
        Once in a while
           I'm still excited by the day's events.
        Always the day involves hurrying,
                trying to catch up
                where I've fallen behind—
                    which is often.
    Before I sleep,
        I thank you for all your generosity toward me,
           for your patience.
        You never tire of my complaints or requests—
           nothing is too preposterous,
                too extreme.
    Like a well-weathered parent,
        you humor my mood swings when no one else will.
    You kiss away the "bumps" and "owies"
        my body and soul endure.
    You laugh at my misadventures;
        you wipe my tears.

Now, Lord, in this quiet time of the day,
    I feel you pull me close.
    I feel your love and healing spill over me.
        How much we have grown together,
            you and I.
        I wonder where we will be in the years to come.
        As hard as this life lesson has been,
            I know one thing:
                I don't want to put you
                on a "back burner" ever again.
        Sharing my life with you, I know, is a necessity—
            one I will not do without.
        In overcoming my loss, I have found a new life—
            a new friend in you.

This night, Lord, I ask you to forgive any pain
    I may have inflicted on others.
    I ask you to forgive any opportunities
        that I may have ignored to share.
        When I could have gone the "extra mile"
            but chose not to,
                forgive me.
        I forgive those who have harmed or slighted me today.
        I lift up to you both my friends and family,
            those dear to me and those who force me
                to grow beyond myself.

I ask for your protection throughout this night, O God.
    Let me find rest and re-creation through my sleep,
        to arise fresh and ready,
        to see what blessings await my awaking.
                                    Amen

For My Family

Lord Jesus,
   It's been said that we can choose our friends,
      but we cannot choose our family.
         Yet, I choose to be friends
            with each member of my family—
               every one, without exception.
   As I heal from my divorce,
      I want my family to heal as well.
         I want us to love, accept,
            and understand one another
               even more than when I was married.
   If I have hurt or damaged any family relationship,
      show me how to repair and rebuild it.
   Show me how to forget my pride and ask forgiveness.
   If I have distanced from family members,
      help me bridge the gap.

I want a healed family, Lord, that shares loving bonds.
   Shape us into a happier,
               healthier,
               holier family—
                  more like the one
                  you lived in at Nazareth.
   Bring us peace and healing.
      Show me how to be an instrument of that peace.
   And thank you, Lord, for the gift of my family.
      With all their flaws and imperfections,
         I love them with all my heart.
                                                Amen

Blessings for My Children

Lord,
    When I'm exhausted,
        all I have to do is remember my children,
            sleeping peacefully—
                and I feel you with us.
    You complete our family; you make it perfect.

Bless my children, Father God.
    Protect them from danger.
        Write their names in the palms of your hands.
        Keep them special.

Bless my children, Mother God,
    Teach them your gentleness,
            your compassion,
            your understanding.
        Touch them with the caresses of your warm breezes.
        Kiss them with a snowflake.
        Warm them with the sun.
        Delight them with your stars.
        Sing them lullabies with the songs of your birds.
        Wake them with the stirring of dawn.

God, our parent, you created us,
    you knew us before we were born.
        Let your love for us overflow,
            spilling over onto others.
                        Amen

Laughter, the Best Prescription

Joyful Friend,
So many times
your blazing anger in the Temple,
your tears at Gethsemane,
your crushed spirit on the cross,
are all we consider.
Living "Catholic" seems synonymous with the phrase,
"This vale of tears."
But, Lord, I'm tired of tears!
It's time to come out of "this vale of tears"
and reach out to the sunshine.
It's time to recall when I smiled,
laughed, and was at peace.
Lord, I'm sure you had humor in your life.
I imagine your twelve adult male friends;
surely, they joked.
Half of them were "old salts,"
and fish tales were the order of the day,
were they not?
Did they amuse you besides confound you?
Did you find yourself drawn into one of their stories,
distracted by their merriment—
while you tried to pray?
Could that be one reason
you had to set time aside for yourself?

You loved little children, Lord!
You must have been touched by their innocence,
their wonderment.

Hearing their stories,
    you must have thrown back your head,
        gusts of laughter pouring out,
        wiping tears of joy from your eyes,
        admiring your Father's creations.
Were you entertained by the stories
    your mother told you?
    Did they bring a tugging smile
    to the corners of your lips?

I hear your stories, Lord, retold in new ways today.
    Parables meant to confound,
        to challenge,
        to portray
            the humor of our humanity.
    To laugh at ourselves is to forgive ourselves,
        to rejoice in our
        common comedy
           called living.
    Everyone messes up.
      No one makes the journey to adulthood
        without taking a few unplanned side trips.
    Help me see my past with a wider vision—
      one that allows me to laugh at my foolish mistakes,
        that says I'm forgiven.
    Let the laughter put my life into perspective.

Teach me how to laugh, Lord—
           just like you did.
                Amen

I've Met Someone

Kind and gracious God,
    I've met someone.
The attraction between us is undeniable.
    When I am with her (him), I feel alive and happy.
    I feel good about myself, too.
    Do I love her (him)?
                I do.
    I must admit the M word has popped into my mind,
        but marriage is not the issue right now.
        In fact, we may never marry.
What this new relationship does mean is that
        I now have a friend,
           someone to talk to and do things with.
    I feel less alone and less lonely now.
My life is already being enriched by this friendship.
    I'm living again and growing again,
        and for that I am so very grateful.

Bless my new friend,
        and help me to look for opportunities
           to be a loving friend in return.
May we learn to enjoy each other
    and enjoy the present moment—
        instead of constantly looking back at the past
        or of being overly concerned about the future.
And if decisions are called for,
        may they be good decisions
    made in accordance to your will
    and plan for our lives.

Lead us, as only you can.
Guide us, as only you can.
Give us wisdom, as only you can.
Place your loving hands on our shoulders and bless us,
          as only you can.
Thank you for the gift of_____.
As our lives and our love begin to blend,
     may you empower us to become the persons
          you have created us to be.

                                        Amen

For Those in Need

Loving God,
   I pause.
      In this brief moment,
         I lift up to you
         those who are hurting and in pain
         from their own experiences of divorce.
   I am so grateful that others have prayed for me—
      so I do the same for those being affected this day,
         this very instant,
            by divorce.

I may never know who they are in life, God.
   You know them—and that is enough.
      Please use this simple prayer
         to bless and help
         even one of these persons.
   Support and strengthen him or her
         just one more day.

Thank you, dear God,
   for the great privilege
      of being able to pray for these my sisters and brothers.
      We share a common bond.
                  Amen

Remarrying

Dear God,
    I believe it is time to move toward remarrying.
      I've learned so much.
      I've learned how to love myself,
             to value myself,
             to appreciate myself,
             to be comfortable with myself.
      I've learned to be calm and peaceful
        when I'm completely alone.

I've matured, God.
    I've grown up a lot.
      At the beginning of creation,
        you said it is not good
        for a person to remain alone.
      With all my heart, I agree.
        I don't want to be alone
        anymore, God.
    I'm ready for a lifelong companion,
      a life-giving relationship.
    I'm ready for another marriage.

As I prepare to begin anew, God, one thing is clear:
    I want you to be the Lord of my new marriage,
      the third Partner in the marriage covenant.
      I know that without a solid spiritual foundation,
        there is no point in remarrying,
          for it will surely turn into more empty pain—
          and I don't ever want that again.

Guide me, good God, to the right partner.
  Bring us together
      and give us the help we need to stay together
      as your whole and healthy children
      in a union blessed and graced by your love.
  Thank you for bringing me
      to this point in the healing process.
          I trust that your providence will provide me
              with a helpmate and soul mate—
          one who will be my faithful friend
              for a lifetime.

I'm ready to remarry, God.
  However and whenever my new marriage comes about,
      I place it completely in your hands.
      Join my new spouse and myself in such a way
      that nothing and no one will ever separate us.
  When it comes to pass,
      may it forever be a marriage in you, the Lord.
                                    Amen

From Tombstone to Steppingstone

Lord God,
   This divorce has been unbearably painful at times.
      For a while,
         I wasn't even sure I would survive.
      Some days
         I still feel like that.
                  Ah,
                  but I don't intend
                  to give up now.

With your help, dear God,
   and with the help of others who care about me,
                  and with me helping me,
         this divorce is not going to become my tombstone.
      Instead,
         I want it to be a steppingstone
         to a new and better life.
                  I'm a survivor.
   An end is always a beginning.
      I want this to be a new beginning,
         leading me forward
                  to exciting new horizons.
   Oh, I'll have bad days as this new life unfolds,
      but I'm no longer afraid of the bad days.
                  With your help,
                  I'll get through them.
   My life is not over—
                  not by a long shot.

You have planted the seeds of hope in my heart,
and that hope tells me that your hand
can bring goodness and order
from the worst possible chaos.

I won't ever let go of that hand, God.
Not ever again.
But I do want to let go—
and let you have your way with my life.
I am turning over everything I am—
and everything I have—to you.
I ask you to manage my life,
even as you transform it
into something much better
than I have ever known.
I want my life to count for something:
to be bigger—not smaller,
more meaningful—not less.

I put my life at your service, God.
Use me, my experiences,
my resources.
Together, we will help others.
Live in and through me,
and grant me the privilege
of doing beautiful things
for you and for your kingdom present in our world.
Send me the people who need me—
and the people I need.

Lord of my destiny, use me!

Amen

Litany of Thanksgiving

Dear God,
> For your help
>> as I fought my way out of the darkness into the light,
>>> Thank you, God.
> For carrying me
>> when I could not walk on my own,
>>> Thank you, God.
> For the healing
>> I have experienced up to this point,
>>> Thank you, God.
> For the fuller healing
>> I have yet to experience,
>>> Thank you, God.
> For those you send to support,
>> affirm, and care for me,
>>> Thank you, God.
> For helping me go on
>> when I could have easily given up,
>>> Thank you, God.
> For the bad days
>> as well as the good days,
>>> Thank you, God.
> For all that I have learned from my divorce experience,
>> and for the knowledge and wisdom
>> that I will share with others,
>>> Thank you, God.
> For no longer being controlled
>> by rage and hatred toward my former spouse,
>>> Thank you, God.

For teaching me how to love,
    respect, forgive, and care for myself,
        Thank you, God.
For providing opportunities to lift burdens from others,
    to help ease their pain,
        Thank you, God.
For no longer being paralyzed;
    for the ability to control my life and move forward,
        Thank you, God.
For moving from pain to peace,
    with your help,
        Thank you, God.
For not giving up on me nor abandoning me
    when I turned away from you,
        Thank you, God.
For your love, mercy, and forgiveness—
    always ready to carry me when I need you most,
        Thank you, God.
For helping me let go of the past
    and believe in a future full of hope,
        Thank you, God.
For teaching me to see endings as beginnings,
    darkness as light,
        Thank you, God.
For transforming me, with your grace,
    from a bitter person to a better person,
        Thank you, God.
For all that has been,
      is now,
      and is yet to be,
        Thank you, good God.
                Amen

Benediction for All Prayers

May you who have been blessed,
   bless others.
May you who have experienced healing,
   become healers yourselves.
May you who have found your strength renewed,
   let someone else draw upon that strength.
May you who have received,
   give in return and not count the cost.

Remember,
   The pain will pass.
   Your brokenness will heal.
   The sun will rise again in your soul.
   Peace will come.
   You will survive.
   You are not alone...ever.
   God walks with you.
   God holds you tenderly and close.
   God's grace will sustain you.
   You are loved.

May you be blessed by God,
   God's Son,
     and their Holy Spirit,
        now and forever.

                    Amen